ELT Development Series

SERIES EDITOR Thomas S. C. Farrell

Task-Based Language Teaching

Farahnaz Faez and Parvaneh Tavakoli

www.tesol.org/bookstore

TESOL International Association
1925 Ballenger Avenue
Alexandria, Virginia, 22314 USA
www.tesol.org

Director of Publishing and Product Development: Myrna Jacobs
Copy Editor: Sarah J. Duffy
Cover: Citrine Sky Design
Interior Design & Layout: Capitol Communications, LLC
Printing: Gasch Printing, LLC

ISBN 978-1-945351-33-4
Library of Congress Control No. 2018952190

Table of Contents

Series Editor's Preface

The English Language Teacher Development (ELTD) series consists of a set of short resource books for ESL/EFL teachers that are written in a jargon-free and accessible manner for all types of teachers of English (native, nonnative, experienced, and novice teachers). The ELTD series is designed to offer teachers a theory-to-practice approach to second language teaching, and each book offers a wide range of practical teaching approaches and methods of the topic at hand. Each book also offers time for reflections for each teacher to interact with the materials presented in the book. The books can be used in preservice settings or in-service courses and can also be used by individuals looking for ways to refresh their practice.

Task-Based Language Teaching, by Farahnaz Faez and Parvaneh Tavakoli, explores various aspects of task-based language teaching (TBLT) and how such an approach can inform language teaching. Faez and Tavakoli outline why TBLT is important, what a task is, how to build a task-based curriculum, and various other factors to consider in TBLT. The authors also include practical implications for language teaching as a guide to using tasks effectively that can be tailored to aspects of teaching and learning such as learner age, proficiency level, aims and needs, class size, and teaching objectives. *Task-Based Language Teaching* is another valuable addition to the literature in our profession and to the ELTD series.

I am very grateful to the authors who contributed to the ELTD series for sharing their knowledge and expertise with other TESOL professionals. It was truly an honor for me to work with each of these authors as they selflessly gave up their valuable time for the advancement of TESOL.

Thomas S. C. Farrell

Preface

Task-based language teaching (TBLT) is gaining popularity among teachers worldwide because it is an effective way to teach a language by engaging learners in authentic and communicative tasks that involve real use of language. TBLT is also suitable for teachers working in various contexts and with learners of different proficiency levels. Teachers have often reported that using tasks in the classroom motivates learners and encourages interaction.

The purpose of this book is to provide a teacher-friendly guide to understanding and implementing TBLT. We discuss the underlying principles of TBLT and highlight how tasks can help promote teaching and learning in language classrooms. Because TBLT has been conceptualized in the field in several ways, we explain the different dimensions and perspectives rather than emphasizing one position over the other. We also summarize the essential pedagogical implications presented in the research.

Chapter 1 provides a rationale for using TBLT, presents its history, and discusses TBLT and its principles. Chapter 2 defines what a task is, discusses task features and types, and outlines the different approaches to TBLT. Chapter 3 summarizes key features of a task-based curriculum and syllabus, presents task cycles, discusses teachers' and students' roles in TBLT, and outlines task-based language assessment goals. Chapter 4 helps teachers evaluate tasks from a practical perspective and highlights key factors to consider. Chapter 5 overviews some of the important practical implications of research in TBLT for language teaching. Finally, Chapter 6 concludes by presenting the strengths and challenges of implementing TBLT.

CHAPTER 1

Why TBLT?

TBLT (sometimes called task-based instruction, or TBI) has received a lot of attention from researchers and educators in the last few decades, and its implementation has been an important educational policy initiative around the world. Several countries, such as China, Japan, Hong Kong, Taiwan, New Zealand, Vietnam, and Canada, have introduced TBLT, formally or informally, as a language teaching method to help improve language learning outcomes.

The Common European Framework of Reference (CEFR), introduced in Europe, describes what learners "can do" using the language they are learning at different stages of their language learning process. The CEFR has been translated into 37 languages to date and has been influential beyond its original context of Europe. The CEFR uses "can do" statements to describe language use across five language skills: listening, reading, spoken interaction, spoken production, and writing. Even though the CEFR does not advocate any particular teaching method, its principles and action-oriented approach lend themselves to a task-based language teaching approach (Little, 2006). The influential nature of TBLT is further demonstrated through the findings of a large-scale study that examined teacher reactions to CEFR's task-based approach in French as a second language classrooms in Canada (Faez, Taylor, Majhanovich, Brown, & Smith, 2011), revealing teachers' positive attitudes toward using such activities. As a result of implementing task-based activities, teachers' estimates of their students' abilities to use the target language increased.

The popularity of TBLT stems from the belief that it is an effective way to engage learners in language learning by providing them with opportunities for authentic use of language in the classroom. Indeed, tasks can provide frameworks that support many of the key elements understood to enhance language acquisition and facilitate effective instruction: negotiation of meaning, output hypothesis, and learner autonomy (Shehadeh & Coombe, 2010).

- *Negotiation of meaning:* Although Long (1985) emphasizes the importance of language input that is understood by the learner, he notes that exposure to the language is not sufficient. Equally important are opportunities to interact and negotiate meaning, which draw learners' attention to properties of the language that are essential for language learning. TBLT provides opportunities for comprehensible input and negotiation of meaning.

- *Output hypothesis:* Swain (1995, 2000) emphasizes that learner output of the target language plays a significant role in the language acquisition process. She argues for *collaborative dialogue* that promotes interaction and dialogue with others in the classroom. TBLT emphasizes interaction and provides excellent opportunities for collaborative dialogue.

- *Learner autonomy:* Recent language teaching approaches emphasize the importance of learner autonomy—learners' ability to take charge of their own learning (Little, 2011). TBLT provides rich opportunities for promoting learner autonomy in the classroom.

REFLECTIVE QUESTIONS

- What is your understanding of TBLT? What have been your experiences with it?

- What excites you about this approach to language teaching? What concerns you about this approach?

History of TBLT

TBLT is not a new approach to language teaching. For example, Prabhu used a task-based approach in secondary classrooms in India as early as 1979. TBLT emerged as a result of applied linguists' and language teachers' dissatisfaction with traditional methods in which language was predominantly taught explicitly and decontextualized as a system of rules and elements such as grammar and vocabulary. There were concerns that these approaches were inconsistent with how people really learn a language (e.g., Long, 1985). Learners were exposed to uncommon language examples and were expected to produce error-free language at a very early stage. Traditional methods of teaching often resulted in learners' knowing the rules but not knowing when or how to apply them in context. In natural processes of language learning, such as children learning their first language or adult immigrants learning a second language outside of school, individuals do not, for the most part, learn language rules. Instead, they learn how to use the language to communicate their intended message and to exchange and understand ideas, thoughts, and feelings.

The introduction of communicative competence and communicative language teaching (CLT) in the 1970s emphasized the shift to base language teaching on communication in social contexts. Several advancements in understanding the nature of language and its acquisition over the years led to what we now call the communicative approach. Language teaching methods are generally informed by a theory of language and a theory of learning (Richards & Rogers, 2001). The theory of language identifies what constitutes language in that approach, and the theory of learning identifies how language is learned. CLT has been described as an approach and not a method (Richards & Rodgers, 2001) since it provides a broad theoretical position about the nature of language (communicative competence), but not much attention has been given to a theory of learning.

TBLT is an extension of CLT in that its theory of language is similar to CLT but provides much more attention to the theory of learning. The underlying principles about the nature of language in TBLT can be summarized as follows:

- Language is a means of communication even if limited linguistic resources are used.
- Language is a means for making meaning.

- Language is a tool for attaining real-world goals.
- Lexical chunks are essential to communication and language learning, emphasizing the significance of vocabulary knowledge and formulaic chunks.

In TBLT, a theory of learning is informed by psycholinguistics, interactional, and sociocultural principles (Robinson, 2003; Skehan, 2018). Here are some of the key tenets of the TBLT perspective on learning:

- Interaction and negotiation of meaning through tasks provide rich opportunities for language learning.
- Language learning is, at least to some extent, an internal process where meaning is constructed by the learner, not the teacher.
- Using existing cognitive, social, and pedagogic resources effectively promotes learning.
- Language learning develops gradually.
- Language learning is facilitated when learners' attention is on completing goal-oriented, real-world activities.
- Learning takes place by doing. Tasks provide opportunities for learning by practicing communicative uses of language.
- Tasks help learners notice the gap in their language knowledge and skills.
- Tasks enhance learners' confidence and willingness to communicate.

REFLECTIVE QUESTIONS

- Which principle(s) about the nature of language in TBLT draws your attention? Why?
- How might assumptions about how language is learned influence language instruction?

What is TBLT?

TBLT has drawn, to a great extent, on the findings of research in second language acquisition. There is general agreement among second language acquisition researchers and teacher educators that instruction is most effective when its focus is primarily meaning-based and supplemented by timely attention to language forms. As such, tasks provide many opportunities for meaningful communication and language use. Similar to CLT, TBLT has been interpreted differently by scholars, and it may mean different things to different people. In essence, however, TBLT is a language teaching approach in which the focus of instruction is using language to do meaningful tasks that resemble the type of activities learners need to do in their real life. While the correct use of language is important and expected to emerge gradually, in TBLT the priority is being able to communicate meaning in a way that the intended message is understood despite learners' limited knowledge of the language. D. Willis and Willis (2007) argue that one of the most valuable aims of TBLT is to give learners "the confidence and willingness to have a go, even if their language resources are limited" (p. 2).

Here are some of the key principles of TBLT:

- Students' needs are central to determining the content of the curriculum.
- Communicative tasks are the key unit for language teaching and learning.
- Learners learn the language by using it.
- Meaning-making should be the primary focus of instruction.
- Focus on form is secondary to meaning and should be provided as needed.
- Tasks are classroom activities that resemble the type of activities learners need to do in their lives outside the classroom.

REFLECTIVE QUESTIONS

- What are some of the strengths of TBLT?
- What are some of the potential weaknesses of TBLT?
- What are some of the challenges of implementing TBLT in your context? How can you overcome these challenges?

CHAPTER 2

What Is a Task?

Now that we have reviewed the underlying principles and assumptions of TBLT, a key question to address is what constitutes a task. Tasks have been defined in numerous ways, and there are several competing definitions of what constitutes a task. But at the core, a task is a classroom activity that requires students to use language in a meaningful, communicative way to achieve an outcome. Some examples of tasks include planning an itinerary for a trip, writing a complaint e-mail/letter about bad service, and preparing an invitation for a party.

Several scholars have provided their definitions of a task:

- Long (1985, p. 89): A task is a piece of work undertaken for oneself or for others, freely or for some reward. Tasks are things people do in everyday life—painting a fence, dressing a child, or borrowing a library book.

- Skehan (1998, p. 95): A task is an activity in which meaning is primary; there is some communication problem to solve; there is some sort of relationship to comparable real-world activities; task completion has some priority; and the assessment of the task is in terms of outcome.

- Bygate, Skehan, and Swain (2001, p. 11): A task is an activity which requires learners to use language, with an emphasis on meaning, to attain an objective.

- D. Willis and Willis (2001): Tasks are used by learners for a communicative purpose to achieve an outcome.

- Nunan (2004, p. 9): A task is a piece of classroom work that involves learners in comprehending, manipulating, producing, or interacting in the target language while their attention is focused on mobilizing their grammatical knowledge in order to express meaning. The intention is to convey meaning rather than to manipulate form.

- Bygate (2016, p. 381): Tasks are classroom activities in which learners use language "pragmatically," that is, "to do things," with the overriding aim of learning language.

REFLECTIVE QUESTIONS

- How would you define a task?

- Review the definitions above and identify what features are commonly used to characterize a task.

Task Features

According to Ellis (2009), a task has the following characteristics:

- The primary focus should be on meaning(i.e., learners should be concerned mainly with processing the semantic and pragmatic meaning of utterances).

- There should be some kind of gap (i.e., a need to convey information, to express an opinion, or to infer meaning).

- Learners should largely have to rely on their own resources (linguistic and nonlinguistic) in order to complete an activity.

- There is a clearly defined outcome other than the use of language (i.e., the language serves as the means for achieving the outcome, not as an end in its own right).

Based on these features, Ellis distinguishes a task from a grammar exercise by arguing that a task fulfills all above-mentioned criteria, whereas a grammar exercise may satisfy only a few of the criteria.

However, it is important to recognize that distinguishing a task from an activity is not black and white, but instead a matter of degree. An emphasis on meaning plays a central role in characterizing a task. Based on the definitions and characteristics above, D. Willis and Willis (2007) suggest asking the following questions to determine how task-like an activity is. The more certain we are about answering yes to these questions, the more task-like the activity. These questions can guide us in designing tasks for our classroom:

- Does the activity engage learners' interests?
- Is there a primary focus on meaning?
- Is there an outcome beyond the use of language?
- Is success judged in terms of achieving the outcome?
- Is task completion a priority?
- Does the activity relate to real-world activities?

REFLECTIVE QUESTIONS

- Think of a task-like activity. Use the questions above to determine the extent to which it can be considered a useful task for your classroom.

- How do your personal experiences as a language learner and/or teacher relate to the use of tasks?

Type of Tasks

Tasks have been classified in several ways, and it is useful to see the different dimensions that have been the focus of these categorizations.

Gap tasks. Prabhu (1987) identifies three categories of gap tasks: information, reasoning, and opinion. In an information gap task, learners are missing information that is necessary to complete the task and they need to communicate with a peer. It involves the transfer of information from one learner to another. One example is pair work in which one person has a picture and must describe it to his or her partner, who has to create the same drawing based on the description. A reasoning gap task involves deriving new information from existing information by inferencing, reasoning, and generating relationships and patterns. One example is generating a travel itinerary based on a limited budget and timing constraints. An opinion gap task is an activity that involves identifying and articulating a person's attitudes and preferences for a particular circumstance. An opinion gap task usually involves gathering factual information and forming arguments to justify one's position. A discussion of a social phenomenon, such as capital punishment or tax evasion, would be a good example.

Real-world and pedagogic tasks. Nunan (2004) identifies two types of tasks: real-world and pedagogic. Real-world tasks resemble the tasks (identified in the needs analysis) that learners need to do in their real life. A mock/practice job interview for someone looking for a job is an example of this type of task. Pedagogic tasks do not necessarily resemble real-world tasks; instead, they are designed for classroom purposes. An information gap activity in which the learners need to find out who in the class has the picture of the story read by the teacher is an example of a pedagogic task.

Unfocused and focused tasks. Ellis (2009) categorizes tasks into unfocused and focused. An unfocused task is designed to promote opportunities for general language use. For example, retelling a picture-based story provides learners with an opportunity to use a range of lexical units and grammatical structures to retell the story. On the other hand, a focused task is designed to provide learners with opportunities to use a particular linguistic feature in communication. An example of a focused task is learners using a specific structure or lexical unit repeatedly, perhaps asking their classmates the same question (e.g., "Have you ever been to a museum?"). Both focused and unfocused tasks must satisfy the four criteria Ellis lists for a task (see above). However, in using a focused task in a classroom, learners are not explicitly told what the linguistic focus of the lesson is, and therefore the lesson can be distinguished from a typical grammar exercise.

Closed and open tasks. D. Willis and Willis (2007) distinguish between closed tasks and open tasks. Closed tasks are those in which there is a correct or predetermined response. Open tasks are those in which the outcome cannot be predicted and learners are free to provide whatever outcome they desire.

Cognitive process classification. It is also possible to categorize tasks on the basis of the cognitive processes involved in them. D. Willis and Willis (2007), for example, suggest listing, sorting, matching, classifying, comparing, and problem-solving as examples of different task types. They argue that teachers find this classification helpful as the categories show what kind of cognitive processes and language functions learners will be engaged in. For example, when pairs of learners are asked to discuss and prepare a list of the most important features of a good college, this listing task encourages them to identify and evaluate the key features of a good college, exchange opinions about it, and negotiate with a partner.

REFLECTIVE QUESTIONS

- What types of tasks might you use more often in your classroom? Why?

- What are the strengths and limitations of each type of task?

Approaches to TBLT

Bygate (2016) and Tavakoli and Jones (2018) identify three main approaches to TBLT.

Task-supported teaching. In this approach, tasks are used to complement or support existing structure-based, language-focused approaches to provide an opportunity for communicative language use.

Task-referenced teaching. In this approach, tasks are used "as a way of defining the target abilities which students are intended to develop by the end of each unit or scheme of work" (Bygate, 2016, p. 387). While in this approach a particular teaching method or learning process is not specified, the reference to tasks is believed to encourage students and teachers to use tasks since they are aware that students' performance will ultimately be evaluated based on these tasks.

Task-based teaching. In this approach, the curriculum is designed based on tasks, hence the teaching and learning is derived from tasks instead of linguistic elements. However, task-based teaching does not exclude the use of nontask activities that are aimed at developing accuracy and fluency.

It is also important to note that a common misconception surrounding tasks is that they focus only on oral interaction. However, tasks can include any of the four language skills; in fact, many tasks are integrative and involve more than one skill.

CHAPTER 3

Building a Task-Based Curriculum

In this chapter, we discuss the definitions of tasks and the task types frequently used in language teaching. We examine the development of a task-based curriculum and the role of tasks in it. The purpose of TBLT is to bring authenticity to the classroom and for learners to be engaged in communication that resembles real-world circumstances. Learners need to be exposed to meaningful input, beginning in the early stages of learning. Learners also need to try communicating with whatever limited linguistic resources they have, focusing on getting meaning across rather than producing accurate forms of language. Such opportunities can be created through the use of real-world tasks in classrooms. In task-based curriculum (not task-supported or task-referenced), tasks become the building blocks of the curriculum, and as such, it is possible to design a whole teaching session or syllabus based on the completion and assessment of tasks.

In the design of tasked-based curriculum, educators must recognize that task-based language teaching is a meaning-based approach in which a focus on meaning is the starting point and a focus on language forms follows, if and when needed. D. Willis and Willis (2007) distinguish form-based approaches from meaning-based approaches in language teaching. Form-based approaches focus on making sure learners produce language accurately, whereas meaning-based approaches focus on communicating and getting learners to produce as much language as possible—even if the language forms they produce are not totally accurate. When the focus is on communication, learners naturally focus on language forms by thinking, "How do I say _____?," "What is the English word for _____?," or "What verb form do I use?" Therefore, in meaning-based approaches, the teacher does not control the language used in the classroom and the effectiveness of instruction is evaluated based on students' successful communication in the classroom, not necessarily their accurate use of language.

However, because meaning is often conveyed by the use of language, and lexical chunks and vocabulary knowledge are central to making meaning in a language, it is necessary to encourage students to use their resources—such as their knowledge of the language rules and lexical chunks, their cognitive and interactional skills, and their communication strategies—to complete language tasks. In other words, learners should use whatever is available to them to successfully communicate. And though an emphasis on grammar is subordinate to successful communication, this does not mean that grammar is ignored in TBLT. Guidance toward the acceptable use of language for communication should be provided, but as a secondary focus of successful communication.

The starting point for designing a task-based curriculum is considering the learners' language learning needs. Students' needs often vary, but these are some general needs to consider: Are they studying English for admission to a university? Do they need the language to be able to function in a specific new community such as a child's school or a doctor's office? Do they need more opportunities to practice speaking or writing? Do they need to use formal or everyday language? Will they be using the target language as the language of instruction? Do they need to expand their vocabulary? Do they need to pass a (written or oral) test? These questions can help guide teachers in selecting and adapting tasks for the particular needs of their students.

The majority of language learners aim to learn a language for functional purposes, hence aligning classroom activities to the types of tasks they need to do in real life enhances their motivation. Teachers can conduct a needs analysis by negotiating the curriculum with learners and identifying a list of target tasks that will be the goals of the language learning program.

From the target tasks, a series of pedagogic tasks can be developed. Pedagogic tasks are detailed work plans for the classroom that gradually build up toward approximating the target tasks (Long, 2015). We discuss pedagogic tasks in more detail below.

TBLT Syllabus

A TBLT syllabus differs from conventional language syllabi, in which linguistic features (e.g., grammar, pronunciation) and language skills (e.g., listening, speaking, reading, writing) are specified. A task-based syllabus identifies the tasks that need to be carried out by students in the program. Typically, a task-based lesson does not involve only a single task; instead, it often includes a series of tasks that relate to one another in order to prepare learners to complete a target task. For example, if the target task is for students to plan a farewell party, a series of tasks to prepare them for this task could include (1) preparing a list of invitees, (2) deciding where to have the party, (3) choosing appropriate food for the party, (4) determining who will do what to help with the preparation, (5) preparing a list of grocery items, (6) exchanging recipes, (7) preparing invitation e-mails, and (8) rehearsing small talk.

Once teachers have identified a particular task, they need to adapt the task so that it meets the particular needs of their students. The following steps can be used to develop tasks for use in the classroom:

1. Carry out a needs analysis to identify target tasks for students.

2. Categorize the tasks based on their level of difficulty for the students.

3. From the inventory of tasks, develop pedagogic tasks.

4. Sequence the pedagogic tasks to make a task-based syllabus.

Task Cycle in TBLT

Even though task-based language lessons can take different forms, it is important to plan the task cycle (or implementation of tasks) for any lesson. Various models have been introduced (e.g., Bygate, 1994; Ellis, 2014; Skehan, 2011; D. Willis & Willis, 2007), and what they have in common is a three-stage model: pretask, on-task, and posttask.

Pretask. The purpose of the pretask phase is to prepare students to perform the task and learn the language. During this phase the teacher introduces the topic and engages learners in activities to help them recall or learn words and phrases essential for performance of the task. This includes presenting students with what will be expected of them to complete the task. When teachers explain the nature, relevance to student-identified language learning goals, and purpose of the task, students may be motivated to wholly engage. Other preparations might include introducing background information about the content through listening or reading activities, presenting key vocabulary and phrases, clarifying instructions and expectations, performing a similar task, providing a model, and engaging students in strategic planning.

On-task. This phase includes a three-stage task cycle (J. Willis, 1996). (1) *Task:* Students perform the task in pairs or small groups. The teacher circulates to ensure that students are heading in an appropriate direction. The teacher provides support and clarification as needed, encourages student attempts at communication, and might interrupt the whole class to address an issue that requires attention. (2) *Planning:* Students prepare to present their work to the whole class and comment on how they did the task. This can be done orally or in writing. The teacher provides support and language advice as needed. (3) *Report:* Groups present their report to the class, and the teacher provides feedback on content and language. It is important to note that in TBLT, the teacher does not expect the same outcome for all students but considers a range of possible solutions to the problem at hand.

Posttask. J. Willis (1996) refers to this as the *language focus* phase, in which students have the opportunity to discuss and examine specific features of the task or text they prepared. Students can write down new words and phrases they have learned, and the teacher provides practice activities with new words or provides form-focused instruction. The posttask phase serves two main purposes. First, it enables the teacher to make sure that students have achieved a clear outcome in terms of language use. The teacher can provide feedback and help students self-correct or reshape their output.

Second, when students have had difficulty with a specific language element during the task, this phase provides an opportunity to present form-focused instruction on those elements. The posttask phase also can be used to draw learners' attention to other aspects of their language learning, including reflection on past learning and planning for future learning pathways.

REFLECTIVE QUESTIONS

- How do you currently sequence the activities in your classroom?

- What does the task cycle presented above tell you about how you can sequence activities in your lessons?

Teachers' Role in TBLT

Teachers' primary role in TBLT is to select appropriate tasks for students based on an analysis of their needs and abilities and to develop pretask, on-task, and posttask activities. Another important responsibility of teachers is to ensure that the tasks and their related activities align with teaching objectives. Teachers also monitor student performance, intervene, and provide form-focused instruction as necessary. The following roles have been identified for teachers in TBLT.

Task selector and designer. A main role for the teacher in TBLT is to select, adapt, or create appropriate tasks and develop an instructional sequence that is suitable to students' needs and language ability.

Task (cycle) planner. The teacher plans the three stages of the task cycle: pretask, on-task, and posttask.

Language resource. The teacher draws student attention to language features and form as necessary at appropriate times, perhaps during the on-task phase or mostly during the posttask phase. This is referred to as *focus on form*. This does not mean providing a grammar lesson before students start the task, but teachers need to provide form-focused instructional strategies as required.

Monitor. The role of the teacher is not only to give students tasks to complete but to watch and monitor their performance and provide input as needed during or after a task.

Assessor. The teacher is also responsible for assessing whether the task has been accomplished and learners have achieved task outcomes.

REFLECTIVE QUESTION

- How are the roles you are currently assuming in your classroom similar to or different from the roles identified for a teacher in TBLT?

Students' Role in TBLT

The roles that students take in TBLT are similar to their roles in any learner-centered or communicative classroom.

Team player. Several tasks, but not all, require students to work in pairs or small groups. Students who are accustomed to working individually or in teacher-fronted classrooms may need to adapt to learner-centered instruction.

Language user. Students are expected to use the target language to complete tasks. For example, they should use language to prepare something (e.g., an application), solve a problem (e.g., find the best hotel), develop a plan (e.g., an itinerary), or complain about something (e.g., quality of food at the cafeteria).

Appraiser. Students should use task performance as an opportunity to notice the gap between what they know and can do with the language and what they are expected to know and do with it. They should be able to appraise their own abilities and detect gaps in their knowledge and attend not only to the content of the tasks but also to the form in which the tasks are conveyed.

Risk-taker. Many tasks require students to understand and use language that they have not fully acquired. Students may have limited linguistic resources and lack prior experiences that would help them preform the task. Indeed, this is the main purpose of these tasks—to challenge students beyond their current ability. Therefore, students need to be comfortable with using various strategies—such as rephrasing, paraphrasing, and asking for clarification and assistance when needed—to overcome their limitations.

Assessment in TBLT

Just as classroom tasks are the main focus of instruction in TBLT, they are the main unit of assessment, too. Generally, the validity of a test is determined based on the extent to which it measures what it is supposed to measure. In this case, the test should measure the successful completion of tasks. Therefore, following the TBLT methodology, the purpose and validity of task-based language assessment lies in the extent to which it can link the test takers' performance on a test to their performance in the real world.

Shehadeh (2013) outlines four features that characterize task-based language assessment (TBLA):

1. TBLA is used mainly as a type of formative assessment in the classroom. The purpose of formative assessment is to monitor student progress so that teaching and learning can be revised and modified for improvement. In contrast, summative assessment is conducted at the end of a teaching cycle, and its purpose is to understand whether students have mastered a topic after instruction.

2. TBLA is a performance-referenced assessment, which means that its purpose is to understand the extent to which students can use the target language in target tasks. It provides information about learners' abilities in using the target language in specific contexts.

3. TBLA is a form of direct assessment, that is, a form of assessment in which students' actual performance is measured through accomplishing target tasks. In indirect measures, inferences about students' abilities are often made based on indirect measures, such as a grammar test to measure language proficiency.

4. TBLA is an authentic form of assessment, which means that it involves real-world target language use or use of language forms that are as close as possible to real-world language.

Many language teachers, language teaching programs, and language testing organizations have moved away from traditional tests, such as those containing grammar, fill-in-the-blank, and multiple-choice items, and are working on the use and development of tasks that can be used in various contexts for different assessment purposes. For example, tasks can be used for diagnostic and placement purposes or to evaluate learners' achievement and proficiency. Using tasks enables the

- assessment of learners' language performance and skills rather than their linguistic knowledge, rewarding learners for what they can do rather than penalizing them for what they cannot do with the language;

- examination of learners' language ability when learners are engaged in authentic and close to real-life activities; and

- encouragement of learners (and teachers) to practice tasks that they will engage in outside the classroom.

CHAPTER 4

Factors to Consider in TBLT

In previous chapters, we discussed different aspects of teaching in a TBLT context, including curriculum, teachers, learners, and assessment. In this chapter, we discuss some of the key factors that should be considered to maximize teaching quality and learning opportunities. Choosing the right task to achieve pedagogic aims and to make the language learning process more efficient and relevant to learners is an extremely important component of TBLT. The following questions are helpful for determining whether a task is suitable for the teaching and learning purposes of a specific context:

- Does the task meet the teaching objectives?
- Does the task help learners achieve their learning needs?
- Does the task prepare learners for using language in real world contexts?
- Is the task interesting, engaging, and motivating?
- Is the task at the right level of difficulty (both cognitively and linguistically)?
- Is the task suitable for the learners?

These questions are often complex and multifaceted; therefore, answering them requires careful and detailed analysis of the task, learning needs, teaching objectives, and the context in which tasks are used. Given the complexity of selecting, designing, and developing appropriate tasks, this chapter identifies key factors—engagement, task goal and task outcome, task input, task type, and task complexity—to help guide the process.

Engagement

The first and perhaps most important factor to consider when choosing or designing a task is to what extent learners will become engaged with the task. Engagement is a particularly important concept since without it, task completion and learning may be difficult to achieve. There are three criteria to consider in order to increase learners' engagement: *relevance*, *interest*, and *authenticity*. First, it is necessary to consider whether completing the task is relevant to learners' language communicative needs (i.e., Is this something they would do in real life?). This clearly involves knowing the learners, their needs, and the context in which they will be using the language outside the classroom. Questions such as whether the learners will use the language for reasons related to work, education, or tourism and leisure can help determine the degree of the task's relevance. Closely linked to the concept of relevance is the question of interest—whether the task engages learners' interests. While it is possible to work with a task that satisfies one characteristic but not the other, tasks are more effective teaching and learning tools if they are both relevant and of interest to learners.

In addition to relevance and interest, teachers need to consider task authenticity, which relates to how closely the tasks approximate what learners do with the language outside the classroom. Authenticity is often considered at two levels: task authenticity and input authenticity. Task authenticity concerns whether the task itself mirrors what learners do in real life (e.g., whether learners would be filling out an application in a real-world situation). Authenticity also relates to the originality of the materials used for language teaching—whether the materials were originally produced for communicative use of language in real life or for pedagogic purposes. Nunan (2004) contends that the main argument is not whether pedagogic materials should be used or not; the main point of the discussion is "what combination of authentic, simulated and specially written materials provides learners with optimal learning opportunities" (p. 49). In other words, materials specifically developed for language teaching are welcome when they are used along with authentic materials and if they create valuable opportunities for learning.

Task Goal and Task Outcome

Another important factor teachers should consider in choosing a task is its goal. When discussing a goal (or purpose, as some may call it), we are in fact asking two fundamental questions about the task: (1) What does the task aim to achieve? (2) What outcome do we expect learners to have fulfilled upon task completion? To answer the first question, it is necessary to think about the different linguistic and pedagogical goals teachers have. This may include the teaching objectives, the kind of linguistic items or language competencies intended, or the cognitive processes learners are expected to engage in during task completion. It is also necessary to consider how the task goal relates to other aspects of the syllabus. Here are some examples of task goals:

- developing confidence in interacting with other speakers in everyday conversations
- developing skills in delivering short talks to a familiar audience
- developing negotiation-for-meaning strategies when talking to others
- obtaining information from written texts for one's personal needs (e.g., finding a doctor)
- developing listening comprehension skills needed to process familiar information
- completing an application form by providing personal information (e.g., a job application)

A task goal helps to identify a task outcome. Task outcomes are concerned with what learners are expected to complete, produce, obtain, or work toward (Ellis, 2003; Skehan, 1998). Learners, for example, could be expected to

- produce a list of colleges in town that provide fine art courses,
- identify the places someone has visited on a map of the neighborhood,
- prepare and deliver a 1-minute talk about their personal interests,
- provide a description of their first day at school,
- discuss with a partner the advantages and disadvantages of living in big cities,
- identify five new words in the lecture and look up the definitions.

As shown in the examples above, task outcomes vary and can take a range of forms, from a simple list to a set of instructions, a short talk, or an essay. When evaluating task outcome, it is also important to think of the expected outcome. (See the Task Complexity section at the end of the chapter for further discussion on discourse domain.)

REFLECTIVE QUESTIONS

- Prepare a list of five task goals relevant to the students you are currently teaching.

- Prepare a list of five task outcomes for the tasks you have used or plan to use in your classroom.

Task Input

Task input, which refers to the nature of the input provided in a task, is another important factor to consider. VanPatten (2003) defines input as the language a learner hears or reads that has some kind of communicative intent. In other words, input contains a message that the learner is supposed to notice. In evaluating task input, teachers should consider the linguistic and nonlinguistic information provided in the task. Input may be linguistic (e.g., written or aural language), pictorial (e.g., video, picture story), numerical (e.g., table, chart), or a combination of these (e.g., slide presentation). In real life, learners are surrounded by language input from numerous sources including signs, commercials, newspapers, flyers, reports, lectures, TV, radio, video, and blogs.

While there are no set rules for what kind of input might be more difficult for learners of different backgrounds and language proficiency levels, learners with limited proficiency may find pictorial and numerical input, as well as texts that are not lexically and syntactically dense, easier to work with. Longer and more linguistically dense texts, complex tables and graphs, and combined inputs may be more appropriate for older, more educated, or more advanced learners. Individual learner differences and preferences may also have an impact on whether learners find different task inputs easy or difficult to work with.

REFLECTIVE QUESTION

- **What forms of task input are appropriate for your students for the five tasks you identified earlier?**

Task Type

Teachers frequently use numerous task types in their teaching. As discussed earlier, there are also different classifications of task types (see Chapter 3 for details). Some teachers may find Prabhu's (1987) classification of *information*, *reasoning*, and *opinion gap* a useful way of distinguishing task types, while others may categorize tasks on the basis of the language skills and functions they promote (e.g., writing, listening). Many teachers also find it useful to evaluate tasks in terms of the cognitive processes they encourage. According to D. Willis and Willis (2007), these are the most frequently used task types:

- listing (e.g., brainstorming, fact finding)
- ordering and sorting (e.g., sequencing, classifying, mind maps)
- matching (e.g., listening/reading, matching)
- comparing (e.g., comparing/contrasting A and B)
- problem solving (e.g., puzzles, working out a solution for X problem)
- sharing personal experience (e.g., storytelling, reminiscences)

- projects and creative tasks (e.g., designing a poster, recording a video)

Another way of categorizing task types is to examine whether learners complete the task alone, in pairs, in small groups, or in larger groups. It's important to stress that tasks can be completed in oral or written forms depending on the goal and the expected outcome. For example, a comparison task (e.g., comparing two local colleges a student researches online) can be done verbally or in writing.

REFLECTIVE QUESTIONS

- It is often possible to use different classifications to describe a task. How would you describe a picture story retelling task where half of the information is owned by one learner and the other half by another learner?

- Which method of classifying tasks appeals to you? Why?

Task Complexity

By far the most researched factor, task complexity allows us to develop insights into how demanding a particular task will be for learners . While there is some disagreement among scholars (e.g., Robinson, 2003; Skehan, 1998) on how to analyze task complexity, from a pedagogic perspective, it is beneficial to evaluate complexity in regard to the *linguistic, cognitive,* and *communicative* demands a task imposes on a learner.

Linguistic demand refers to the range and complexity of the linguistic units that are needed to complete the task. To ensure the task entails the right linguistic demand for learners, teachers may need to consider the range of structures and vocabulary and the complexity and density of the language used in the task input and the expected outcome. Several questions can be asked in this regard:

- What range of grammatical structures are needed to complete the task?

- To what extent are the structures and vocabulary used in a text familiar to learners?

- Is the density of the language that learners are working with at the right difficulty level (i.e., neither too easy nor too difficult)?

The second aspect of complexity is related to the demands of the cognitive processes and cognitive familiarity involved in task completion and outcome achievement. In terms of cognitive processing demands, the questions to ask include the following:

- Is the information presented in the task clearly structured and transparently communicated?

- How much computation and analysis of the information does the task require?

- Is the information provided sufficient, but not too much, for task completion?

Cognitive familiarity refers to learners' familiarity with the task type, the discourse domain (e.g., news, picture description, interview, argument, poems), the topic, and the information provided in the task. When evaluating task familiarity, key questions to ask include the following:

- Is the task topic familiar to learners?

- Is the task content familiar to learners?

- Have learners previously worked with this discourse domain (e.g., picture description)?

The final aspect of complexity, the degree of communicative demand the task imposes on the learner, reflects the conditions under which the task is performed (Skehan, 1998). Time limits and time pressure, learners' role in the task (whether speaker or listener), working independently or with others, who the audience is, and the type of interactions involved (whether it is possible to slow down interaction) are some of the important factors that determine the communicative demands associated with a task. TBLT research has shown that for most learners, time limits, working with a less known audience, and taking a more active role in the task add to the communicative pressure learners experience and report (Ellis, 2005).

REFLECTIVE QUESTION

- How will considerations of task complexity impact the choices you make in terms of task selection, sequencing, and design?

CHAPTER 5

Practical Implications for Language Teaching

In Chapter 4, we summarized some of the key TBLT research findings that have practical implications for language teaching and learning. This body of research suggests that certain task features and implementation conditions create valuable opportunities for learning and help teachers achieve expected learning outcomes. In this chapter, we discuss some of the important pedagogic implications of TBLT research for second language teaching and learning, highlighting task features and implementation conditions that facilitate teaching and promote learning. We discuss each of these task features and conditions from a practical perspective, evaluating the benefits and challenges introduced to classroom language teaching and learning. Although this chapter can be viewed as a guide to using tasks more effectively, we do not suggest that these implications are applicable to all teaching and learning contexts or may equally benefit all learners. We suggest that such implications should be considered in relation to other important aspects of teaching and learning, such as learner age, proficiency level, aims and needs, class size, and teaching objectives.

Planning Time

Planning time is a widely researched task implementation condition shown to help promote task performance and learning. Planning time, often simply called planning, involves providing time to learners before or during task completion to plan what they are going to say or write. From a learning perspective, research in this area has provided solid evidence that giving learners an opportunity to plan has at least three favorable results: (a) promotes immediate learner output, (b) helps enhance learning, and (c) increases learners' positive attitudes toward task performance (Skehan, 2018). The theoretical principle supporting these results comes from psycholinguistic research. This research suggests that the human mind has limited capacity to pay attention to and process complex information, especially when engaged in a demanding activity such as communicating in a second language that has not yet become automatic (Skehan, 1998). Therefore, giving learners time to plan before or during completing the task can help release attentional resources and ease the pressure on their working memory. Planning time also provides learners with opportunities to scan their linguistic resources, identify what they know and can do with their knowledge, identify what they need to know or learn, and eventually pull their knowledge and skills together to complete the task.

Planning time has been of substantial interest to language teachers because it can be an effective pedagogic tool that helps them mediate and scaffold the language learning process. From a teaching perspective, planning time is a valuable instructional tool that encourages learners to pay attention to both form and meaning, and gives teachers an opportunity to monitor what learners know and what they need to know to complete tasks. Planning time also encourages learner autonomy by giving learners a chance to evaluate their abilities and notice the gap between what they can do and what they are expected to do.

Two types of planning are of interest to teachers: pretask and during-task. Pretask planning, whether in the form of asking learners to have a rehearsal before they perform for the class or just to think about and plan for it (strategic planning), is particularly useful for

- attracting learners' attention,
- noticing the gap (between what they can do and what they need to do),

- increasing coherence and structure of task performance, and
- improving fluency.

During-task planning, which gives learners an opportunity to plan as they are engaged in task completion, enables learners to

- monitor their language as they are producing it,
- feel less pressured (as they have more time), and
- pay more attention to the forms of language they are using.

Planning can be done individually or in small groups, or it can be teacher-led. Research shows that individual planning helps promote learners' fluency, group planning increases the range of language used and enriches the content, and teacher-led planning leads learners toward more accurate language use.

Another crucial consideration is how much planning time should be made available to learners. Clearly, the amount of planning time depends on the type, task, and outcome of the task, but as a general rule most studies have shown that planning time should be neither too long nor too short. For example, in a picture story retelling task that requires a 4-minute performance, a 1-minute planning time is too short to be beneficial for learners and a 10-minute planning time may distract learners and disrupt their focus (see Ashcraft, 2014, for a detailed discussion of lesson planning).

REFLECTIVE QUESTIONS

- Providing planning time is not without challenges, especially in large classes. What are some of the challenges that you foresee? What can you do to overcome such challenges?

Task Repetition

Another task condition that helps promote language learning is task repetition, which provides learners with opportunities to repeat the same task two or more times. Ample research in this area suggests that learners benefit from repetition, whether repeating the same task and its content or repeating the same task with different content each time. Like with planning time, the underpinning principle is informed by psycholinguistic studies, highlighting humans' limited attentional resources (Skehan, 1998). During the initial task performance, learners may be too busy to pay enough attention to aspects of form and meaning. Therefore, task repetition can provide them with a valuable opportunity to attend to both form and meaning, evaluate their own performance, and see what changes they need to make to their first performance. Research shows that when learners repeat a speaking task for a second time, they speak more fluently, producing faster and less interrupted speech, and they use a wider range of structures and vocabulary items (de Jong & Perfetti, 2011). Some studies also suggest that the benefits continue even after a third repetition. Task repetition can be combined with other task-related conditions, such as providing planning time between first and second task performance, to achieve pedagogic objectives.

Like planning time, task repetition may add new challenges to classroom teaching. One of the key challenges is that some students may find task repetition unnecessary or boring. One way to reduce the boredom factor and to sustain learners' motivation and engagement is to use different task content in the second or third repetition. Another way to deal with this problem is to ask learners to present the second, third, or fourth repetition to a different interlocutor or audience. Learners should be made aware of the fact that in everyday real life, we repeat many language tasks. Examples of real-life task repetitions include telling friends, family, and colleagues about our holiday when we come back to work; narrating an accident we have witnessed to several people; or providing the same information to different partners in a speed dating game.

REFLECTIVE QUESTIONS

- What challenges does task repetition introduce to large classes? How can you overcome such challenges?

Organization of Information

The organization of information in a task impacts learners and the learning process. Although many aspects of organization of information have been researched in TBLT, for reasons of scope we discuss only five: task structure, amount of information, and immediacy of information, task familiarity, and focus on form.

Task structure. Task structure refers to how task information is presented and organized. Well-structured tasks have been shown to influence learner task performance in systematic and predictable ways. Learners are assumed to have more attentional resources available when the task information is presented in a coherent manner, the organization of the information is easy to understand and follow, and there are explicit steps and procedures for learners to follow in order to complete the task. On the other hand, tasks that require reordering of information, include an unexpected turn of events or presentation of information, and are open to interpretation usually require more attention, and as such may be more demanding for many learners. For example, a well-structured picture story in which the pictures are put in the right order to show the sequence of events is more suitable for learners with limited proficiency than a picture story where the sequence of events needs to change for the story to make sense. With high-level learners or learners who are expected to engage in more demanding and complex tasks, less structured tasks may be appropriate. For example, information may need to be reorganized, some aspects of the task information could be open to personal interpretation, or the sequence of activities can be reshaped. Less structured provide rich opportunities for negotiation of meaning and generate more interaction among learners.

Amount of information. Including the right amount of information in a task is an essential factor for successful task performance and language learning. Too much information and too little information make the task too difficult to complete and minimize opportunities for learning. Like with previous task features, the amount of information teachers provide in a task depends on several factors such as learner age and interest as well as teaching objectives. The amount of information provided closely relates to learners' proficiency level. Learners with lower proficiency may find too much information in a task difficult to handle as they may feel overwhelmed working with a task that requires a lot of attention and effort to process the information.

Immediacy of information. Task completion is facilitated when task information is readily available and accessible to learners. When the core information is available, there is less pressure on learner memory, and as a result, learners can focus on task completion. For example, if they are narrating a picture story, having the story available to learners during task completion provides them with better learning opportunities. Similarly, when writing a financial report based on data presented in a graph, learners need to have the graph available while writing the report. However, at times teachers may decide that some information should not be available if they want to make a task more challenging for more advanced learners or when task completion is part of a class contest or quiz.

REFLECTIVE QUESTIONS

- In what ways can organization of information help you develop more suitable tasks? Is organization of information more relevant to speaking, writing, reading, or listening tasks?

Task familiarity. Being familiar with task type, task content, and task instruction benefits task performance. Working with familiar tasks, content, and information allows learners to use their cognitive and linguistic resources more effectively. This does not mean that a less familiar task should not be used. Sometimes teachers decide to expose learners to a more challenging task so that their knowledge and skills are stretched and new knowledge or skills are developed. Therefore, task familiarity can be considered when ranking tasks in the degree of their difficulty and challenge. Task familiarity can also be manipulated to keep learners interested and engaged. For example, in mixed-ability groups, more proficient learners can be kept more actively engaged in the task when working with unfamiliar content and topics, while the less proficient learners work with familiar content and/ or topics.

Focus on form.[1] Although the primary focus of a task is on communicating meaning, task completion should provide opportunities to bring or direct learners' attention to form and to the relationship between form and meaning. TBLT research (Long, 1985, 2015; Nunan, 2004) suggests that the focus-on-form opportunity is a very useful learning moment when learners can consolidate their implicit learning by receiving explicit instruction. To express meaning, learners need to think about what language to use and how to use it. This may involve questions about the choice of lexical or structural

---

[1] Please note that focus on *form* is different from focus on *forms*. The former is a key principle in TBLT that suggests form is important in the context of communicating meaning, and as such one or more forms can be identified during or immediately after task completion to draw learners' attention to. With focus on forms, however, learners' primary attention is on examining and learning the forms of language rather than on exchanging meaning.

units, pronunciation of words, expressions and sentences, spelling questions, or specific questions about grammatical units needed to complete the task. Although focus on form is primarily driven by learners and their needs, teachers can be proactive in identifying items for focus on form before and during task completion. Undoubtedly, the choice of lexical and structural units or the need for correcting a specific pronunciation or spelling point naturally is driven by task design and task content. Still, teachers can identify words, phrases, lexical chunks, pronunciation, spelling, and grammatical points that may need to be discussed or tended to during the on-task or posttask phase of the teaching cycle. While students are completing the task, teachers can identify error correction points, such as frequent errors or errors that impede communication, to discuss when they focus on form. Teachers can also prepare and develop some form-focused activities that can help attract learners' attention to aspects of form that have been shown to be difficult or problematic during task completion.

See Appendix A for a sample TBLT lesson plan.

REFLECTIVE QUESTIONS

- Some learners have keen interest in learning about language forms and may ask you to spend time focusing on a range of forms that may not relate to the task you have just completed. How would you deal with such interest?

- How much class time do you think should be spent on focus on form?

CHAPTER 6

Conclusion

The main purpose of this book has been to introduce TBLT, its rationale and principles, and to highlight the key merits and challenges it introduces to teaching English to speakers of other languages (TESOL). Although we mainly discussed using TBLT in TESOL contexts, we believe that the principles apply to many other language teaching contexts. We reviewed some practical implications of the findings of TBLT research for classroom teaching and learning, and we offered a list of factors that can be considered when choosing and designing tasks. In our discussion, we highlighted the importance of using language tasks for the purpose of communication, and we emphasized the significant role of tasks in language teaching to provide learners with opportunities to use language for meaning making and communication purposes.

It is necessary to note that tasks are frequently used for different language skills and are not restricted to promoting only oral–aural skills. Although many tasks are designed to engage in one particular skill, such as speaking or writing, in reality most tasks involve more than one language skill as they start from one and move to integrate others. For example, a task that begins with listening may require speaking and end with a writing component.

We suggested that adopting a task-based approach to instruction not only facilitates language learning but also motivates both teachers and learners. Our discussion showed that tasks promote learning and provide

- a suitable context for negotiating meaning and interacting with other users of the language,

- opportunities for learners to test what they know and to notice what they need to know to complete the task,

- rich opportunities to put what learners know into practice spontaneously,

- a chance to learn from how others express similar meanings.

In order to ensure the key principles of TBLT are adhered to, you can remind yourself of the following:

- Language learning starts from a focus on meaning, and therefore communicating meaning is the starting point and primary focus.

- A focus on form is also important when it helps promote meaning.

- Use of tasks should mirror what learners do in their real life.

- Use of language is complemented by inviting learners to use other resources and tools that are available to them.

- Task completion is assessed in terms of the expected outcomes (regardless of what forms have been used).

We discussed the key features of a task and how to distinguish a task from a traditional language teaching exercise. A task embraces the following:

- a primary focus on meaning

- a gap (e.g., information, communication, reasoning) that requires communication

- a need for learners to use their nonlinguistic as well as linguistic resources to complete the task (e.g., make an argument, draw a map, solve a problem)

- a communicative outcome beyond the use of language (e.g., a list of criteria for a good school, a decision about something, a map drawn).

We explained that three kinds of syllabi use tasks: task-based, task-supported, and task-referenced (see Tavakoli & Jones, 2018, for further discussion). While many teachers use tasks frequently alongside other approaches to support their teaching objectives, in some language teaching programs tasks are the building blocks of the syllabus and all the teaching objectives are built on tasks. From a methodological perspective, whether you use tasks in a task-based or task-supported syllabus, here are some key principles to follow when using tasks:

- Choose tasks carefully on the basis of learners' needs beyond the classroom context.
- Use tasks as a unit of teaching.
- Evaluate tasks not only in terms of the linguistic requirements they impose on the learners, but in terms of their interactional, sociolinguistic, and cognitive demands.
- Identify specific outcomes that learners need to achieve upon task completion.
- Be prepared for a focus on form when and if the need arises.

From a developmental perspective, we suggest that using tasks

- provides opportunities to scaffold learning through the pretask, on-task, and posttask cycles;
- helps learners move more freely in their zone of proximal development;
- encourages learners to prioritize fluency while attending to accuracy; and
- helps learners become more autonomous and take responsibility for their learning.

We also discussed the limitations and challenges that adopting a TBLT approach may introduce to language teaching. Here are some of the key challenges teachers have experienced when using a TBLT approach:

- choosing and designing tasks that meet learners' needs
- examining tasks beyond the linguistic requirements and identifying their interactional, sociolinguistic, and cognitive demands

- striking a balance between a focus on meaning and a focus on form
- using tasks in large classes and with learners who are in favor of more traditional approaches to language teaching and learning

We wrote this book with TESOL teachers in mind. However, given the diversity of teacher professional needs, the range of contexts, and different learner needs, aims, ages, and proficiency ranges, we should acknowledge that the principles and criteria discussed in this volume may not apply to all TESOL or other language teachers. In light of the narrow scope of the book, we are aware that our discussion may also be limited in terms of its application to other neighboring areas of language teaching, such as English for academic purposes, English for specific purposes, and English as an additional language. These restrictions aside, we believe the book is a useful addition to the TESOL series and hope that it will be used by many teachers as an introduction to the field of TBLT.

Appendix A

Sample TBLT Lesson Plan
Gonzalo Galian Lopez, University of Reading

Context: Adult learners of mixed nationalities at B1 level, private language school in Reading, England

Topic: Transport; the best way to get around a city

Background: Learners have been learning vocabulary related to the topic of transport and grammar to make comparisons (comparatives and superlatives). The tasks in this lesson provide opportunities for learners to put this language into use in meaningful contexts.

Target task: Explaining and comparing ways of getting around a city (orally and in writing)

Task sequence

1. Introduce the topic and aims of the lesson, and ask the class to brainstorm vocabulary about forms of transport that they can use when they visit a new city.

2. Tell learners that their partners will be visiting their hometowns and that they should prepare a list of transportation methods for getting around during their stay. Ask learners to talk about three or four transportation forms and to consider their advantages and disadvantages so that their partners can choose the most suitable methods. Give leaners the following chart so that they can make some preparation notes for the task.

_____		_____	
+	–	+	–
_____		_____	
+	–	+	–

3. In pairs, have learners present ways of getting around their hometowns. When listening to their partners, they should decide which form of transport would be most suitable for them and why. Follow this with a brief whole-class discussion in which some learners explain their choices.

4. Have the class brainstorm ways of getting around London and then discuss the following (from *English File Intermediate* [Oxenden, Latham-Koenig, & Seligson, 2013]) in small groups.

Look at the four forms of public transport in London. Which one do you think is probably...?

- the most expensive
- the healthiest
- the best if you want to see the sights of London
- the safest to use late at night

5. Ask learners to read the text at the end of this document (adapted from *English File Intermediate*) to check their predictions. Tell them not to write anything in the gaps at this stage. The class can subsequently check answers as a group.

6. Have learners cover the text, and display the following fill-in-the-blank sentences from the text on a PowerPoint slide. Ask learners to try to remember the missing words (all comparatives and superlatives). They should first think about the missing words alone and check their answers in small groups before the whole class checks the answers together. Then as a class, briefly discuss why comparatives and superlatives could be useful for the target task.

- The tube is _____ _____ way to get around the city.

- _____ _____ way to use the underground is to get an Oyster card.

- Buses can be _____ _____ the underground if there isn't too much traffic.

- _____ _____ way to use the buses is to just use your Oyster card.

- Bikes are now _____ _____ _____ ever in London.
- Mini-cabs are _____ _____ _____ black taxis.
- Taxis or mini-cabs are probably _____ _____ way to travel late at night.

7. To conclude the lesson, as a class, briefly review the aims of the lesson and the language that received attention.

8. Ask learners to repeat the target task for homework. This time, tell them to do it in writing and with some focus on form (vocabulary and grammar).

Transport in London

London Underground (The Tube)

This is the quickest way to get around the city and there are many underground stations all over London. The cheapest way to use the underground is to get an Oyster card. This is like a phone card. You put money on it, and then top it up when you need to, and then you use it every time you get on or off the Tube. You can buy Oyster cards at tube stations and in newsagents.

Buses

They can be quicker than the underground if there isn't too much traffic. The easiest way to use the buses, like the underground, is to just use your Oyster card. You can also buy tickets from machines next to the bus stops. On some buses you can buy a ticket with cash when you get on the bus. Some of the buses operate 24 hours a day, so you can also use them late at night. Travelling on the top of a double-decker bus is also a good way to see London.

Bikes

Bikes are now more popular than ever in London, especially with tourists and people who want to be fit. There are quite a lot of cycle lanes, and bikes that you can hire, nicknamed "Boris Bikes" after Boris Johnson, the mayor of London. You can use your credit card to hire a bike, and the first 30 minutes are free.

Taxis

London's black taxis are expensive, but they are comfortable and the taxi drivers know London very well. You normally tell the driver where you want to go before you get in the taxi. Mini-cabs are normal cars which work for a company, and which you have to phone. They are much cheaper, but make sure you use a licensed company. Taxis or mini-cabs are probably the safest way to travel late at night.

References

Ashcraft, N. (2014). *Lesson planning*. Alexandria, VA: TESOL.

Bygate, M. (1994). Adjusting the focus: Teacher roles in task-based learning of grammar. In M. Bygate, A. Tonkyn, & E. Williams (Eds.), *Grammar and the language teacher* (pp. 237–259). Hemel Hempstead, England: Prentice Hall International.

Bygate, M. (2016). Sources, developments and directions of task-based language teaching. *Language Learning Journal, 44,* 381–400.

Bygate, M., Skehan, P., & Swain, M. (2001). *Task-based learning: language teaching, learning and assessment.* London, England: Longman.

De Jong, N., & Perfetti, C. A. (2011). Fluency training in the ESL classroom: An experimental study of fluency development and proceduralization. *Language Learning, 61,* 533–568.

Ellis, R. (2003). *Task-based language learning and teaching.* Oxford, England: Oxford University Press.

Ellis, R. (2005). *Planning and task performance in a second language.* Amsterdam, Netherlands: John Benjamins.

Ellis, R. (2009). Task-based language teaching: Sorting out the misunderstandings. *International Journal of Applied Linguistics, 19,* 221–246.

Faez, F., Taylor, S., Majhanovich, S., Brown, P., & Smith, M. (2011). Teacher reactions to CEFR's task-based approach for FSL classrooms. *Synergies Europe, 6,* 109–120.

Little, D. (2006). The Common European Framework of Reference for Languages: Contents, purpose, origin, reception and impact. *Language Teaching, 39*(3), 167–190.

Little, D. (2011). The common European Framework of reference for languages: A research agenda. *Language Teaching, 44*, 381–393.

Long, M. (1985). Task, group and task-group interaction. *University of Hawaii Working Papers in ESL, 8*, 1–26.

Long, M. (2015). *Second language acquisition and task-based language teaching.* London, England: Willey.

Nunan, D. (2004). *Task-based language teaching: A comprehensive revised edition of designing tasks for the communicative classroom.* Cambridge, England: Cambridge University Press.

Oxenden, C., Latham-Koenig, C., & Seligson, P. (2013). *English file intermediate* (3rd ed.). Oxford, England: Oxford University Press.

Prabhu, N. (1987). *Second language pedagogy.* Oxford, England: Oxford University Press.

Richards, J., & Rodgers, T. S. (2001). *Approaches and methods in language teaching: A description and analysis* (2nd ed.). New York, NY: Cambridge University Press.

Robinson, P. (2003). The cognition hypothesis, task design and adult task-based language learning. (2003). *Second Language Studies, 21*(2), 45–107.

Shehadeh, A. (2013). *Task-based language assessment: Components, development, and implementation.* Cambridge, England: Cambridge University Press.

Shehadeh, A., & Coombe, C. (2010). *Applications of task-based learning in TESOL.* Alexandria, VA: TESOL.

Skehan, P. (1998). *A cognitive approach to language learning.* Oxford, England: Oxford University Press.

Skehan, P. (2011). *Researching tasks: Performance, assessment and pedagogy.* Shanghai, China: Shanghai Foreign Language Education Press.

Skehan, P. (2018). *Second language task-based performance: Theory, research, assessment.* London, England: Routledge.

Swain, M. (1995). Three functions of output in second language learning. *Principle and Practice in Applied Linguistics: Studies in Honour of HG Widdowson, 2*(3), 125–144.

Swain, M. (2000). The output hypothesis and beyond: Mediating acquisition through collaborative dialogue. In J. Lantolf (Ed.), *Sociocultural theory and second language learning* (pp. 97–114). Oxford, England: Oxford University Press.

Tavakoli, P., & Jones, R. (2018). *An overview of approaches to second language acquisition and instructional practices.* Cardiff, Wales: Welsh Government.

VanPatten, B. (2003). *From input to output: A teacher's guide to second language acquisition.* New York, NY: McGraw-Hill.

Willis, J. (1996). *A framework for task-based teaching.* Harlow, England: Longman.

Willis, D., & Willis, J. (2001). Task-based language learning. In R. Carter & D. Nunan (Eds.), *The Cambridge guide to teaching English to speakers of other languages* (pp. 173–179). Cambridge, England: Cambridge University Press.

Willis, D., & Willis, J. (2007). *Doing task-based teaching: A practical guide to task-based teaching for ELT training courses and practising teachers.* Oxford, England: Oxford University Press.